THE MEANING OF
VIKTOR E FRANKL

The Meaning of Viktor E Frankl

An Unofficial Biography of a Man

Who Searched for The Meaning of

Life

Author: Oswald Eakins

DEDICATION

Dedicated to Almighty.

DISCLAIMER

Although the author and publisher have made every effort to ensure that the information in this book was correct at press time, the author and publisher do not assume and hereby disclaim any liability to any party for any loss, damage, or disruption caused by errors or omissions, whether such errors or omissions result from negligence, accident, or any other cause.

Contents

Acknowledgments

Greatly thankful to everyone for their immense
support for the release of this book.

Finding Meaning in Suffering

Once there was a man who was unable to cope with the devastating loss of his beloved wife. He was slowly slipping into the dark, bottomless pit of depression. Nothing and no one could assuage his pain. His heart and soul were awash with grief. The hollow comforting words of his friends failed to touch his shattered heart. He was hopeless and had lost all meaning to his life. One morning he decided to get clinical help to treat the malaise of his heart. He poured out his heart to the doctor. The doctor listened to him empathetically. The man was weary of his long and lonely future. Why should he live and for whom? What was the purpose of living with no one to love? Life had suddenly lost all meaning. The doctor acknowledged the man's irreplaceable loss, that the meaninglessness of life was frustrating, but he asked him one question, and in that second the man was changed, his life had transformed.

The doctor asked- imagine a scenario where instead of your wife, you had died, how do you think your wife would have survived the loss? He was quick to reply that if such an event had occurred, she would have been traumatized and suffered immensely. The doctor asked- in that case, by suffering the way you do now, aren't you relieving her of the suffering? The man stopped crying. It was as if time had frozen his tears. After a few seconds of ruminating, he turned back and left a changed man. He never saw the doctor again. He needed no healing because his suffering just got a meaning. The doctor didn't change the situation, nor was he capable of erasing the man's grief, but he had changed the man's attitude towards the suffering. The man had a reason to live on despite his grief. It gave him a purpose to carry on. The thought that by suffering he was relieving his wife was enough to keep him carry on with his life. The doctor was Viktor Frankl, an Austrian psychiatrist and the man was one of his patients.

Man's Search for Meaning

Man's Search for Meaning is a book by Holocaust survivor Viktor Frankl. It is a psychological memoir of the author, a meditation on his life as a prisoner in Auschwitz, Hitler's most infamous concentration camp during World War Two. The book chronicles his horrific experiences at the concentration camps. At Dachau and Auschwitz, Frankl was savagely beaten and tortured, stripped of his identity, worked to death, sparsely fed and clothed even during the brutal winters. He suffered from debilitating illnesses, frostbitten toes, and was subjected to vermin and edema. The image that he evokes of the death camps and its horrors is sure to send shivers down one's spine. The chilling details of everyday life in the camp are unimaginable. Frankl lost his father, mother, brother, and wife at the camp. He saw death, debilitation, and starvation all around. The Nazi concentration camp was a place of evil. People or fellow inmates dropped dead daily, or they were ruthlessly shot at for no particular reason. Hopelessness thrived. Depression and darkness loomed large in the dark corridors of the camp and yet Frankl managed to keep his hope alive. He defied all circumstantial challenges and overcame all hurdles to achieve "meaning" or "purpose" in life even in the most despairing times and situations. How did he do that?

First, Frankl was unaware of his wife's death at that time. The vision of his wife, memories of him conversing with her gave him the reason to live on despite the drudgery. He often laid impoverished and famished on the wooden barracks and conjured out her image in his mind. Her thoughts and the idea of meeting her once again kept him afloat on those freezing winter nights. Even when his stomach grumbled ceaselessly, despite his toes and fingertips being frostbitten, and in spite of the exhaustion of a hard day's labor, and despite all the despair and hopelessness all around, Frankl managed to keep the embers of hope alive in his heart. He fed them with the fires of love. The love for his wife, the thought of seeing her once again kept him going no matter what. Frankl's greatest triumph is that the Nazis couldn't kill his spirits.

When Frankl entered the camp in 1942, he had a manuscript of a book he had written on psychotherapy. Hitler's "brown shirts" had confiscated and destroyed it. Frankl was deeply hurt but he knew he had to write it again, if not for himself, for humanity. Frankl vowed that he would write the book once liberated. The fact that he believed and foresaw a day when he and his fellow inmates would be liberated was in itself a sign of resilience. Many were so depressed and in an abysmal mental and physical state that they had given up all hopes. They had forsaken the last vestiges of being a human. Many couldn't bear the torture and pain meted out daily and chose suicide. Frankl's own friends often contemplated the idea of self-annihilation. He talks about this incident in the book.

Frankl saw two of his friends deep in conversation with each other. When asked what they were so keenly discussing, one of them said they were thinking of ending this ceaseless suffering. Frankl goaded them to stop thinking of what they can do in life and start thinking about what life expects of them. To this question, one man replied with tears of joy in his eyes that he loved his daughter-who was able to escape to the States before being rounded up for incarceration- so much that he cannot wait to see her again and hold her in his embrace for one last time. The other one looked happy too. Frankl urged him to talk about his life's expectations. The man was a doctor, and he had the ambition to publish books that will help many people. His intellectual and academic wealth of knowledge had to be written and made available to humanity.

Two hopelessly depressed people were on the brink of committing suicide. Frankl had not changed their situations. They remained in the same appalling plight, but he managed to convince them that despite the morass they were in, they could still change their attitude towards it. Frankl made them see the meaning in life's sufferings. He showed them that even in the grimmest situation, hope lived. We only had to see it. Something or someone to look forward to in the future was the impetus to live, despite the unpleasant situations. Frankl's lessons in psychotherapy were written decades ago and yet it holds water to this day. He discovered logotherapy, a means of using the purpose in life to overcome all grief. In his book, Frankl argues that the central human motivational force is the search for meaning. As different from Sigmund Freud's psychoanalytical theory which dwells on the fact that the human mind consists of the conscious part and the unconscious part and all his healing were by accepting that every individual had three elements, namely, the ego, the identity, and the superego. Freudian theories involve life and death instincts, psychosexual analysis, and defense mechanisms in humans. All the three elements of a human being together are responsible for very complex human behavior. The second school of Viennese psychotherapy is proposed by Alfred Adler. According to Adler, every human being has an innate inferiority complex. His entire life is to overcome this inadequacy, the eternal "striving for superiority". He espoused that this strife to achieve superiority was the driving force for all human behaviors, emotions, and thoughts. Frankl's psychoanalysis, logotherapy was introduced as the third branch of psychotherapy. Frankl has published 35 books. Man's Search for Meaning is an autobiographical rendition of his accounts, studies, and logotherapy techniques. Originally published in German, by the time of his death in 1997, the book had sold 10 million copies in 24 different languages worldwide. A reader survey conducted in 1991 by the Library of Congress had asked readers to name a book that made a difference in their life and the results showed Man's Search for Meaning in the list of most influential books in the United States of America.

To Auschwitz...

Frankl was just one of the survivors of the horrors of concentration camps. As the Second World War raged on, Hitler had come up with a vile plan and proposed it as the "final solution to the Jewish problem"- the building of concentration camps. Normal happy people who lived a decent life until then were suddenly facing extermination. Jews were ostracized, their shops and buildings vandalized, their children thrown out of schools, elderly and young targeted, humiliated, and beaten up in public places. At that time, only men in the Jewish faith grew a beard, especially the older men so it was easier to spot them. They would be cornered, their possessions taken, and if even a semblance of resistance was shown, they would be brutally beaten. One man had sowed the seeds of hatred and managed to convince a whole population that Jews were "cursed" and that they deserved to be ill-treated, and demonized. Large-scale propaganda was rampant. Huge hoardings proclaimed the need to annihilate Jews. It was a grand scale ethnical cleansing. Hitler's pathological hatred for Jews is known, but he also despised the gays, the blacks, the Slavs, and the disabled. As Hitler's war machines rampaged through Western Europe, more and more Jews were crammed into trains and sent off to hell on earth. Within a few months after Hitler was appointed Germany's chancellor, hundreds of concentration camps had mushroomed. Upon reaching the station, the victims are segregated and sorted. The heart-wrenching separation of young children and infants from their mothers is heart-breaking. Eva Mozes Kor is one of the many survivors of the Holocaust who revisited Auschwitz, to the place where she last saw her mother. Eva, an octogenarian at the time of her visit couldn't resist the hot tears brimming in her eyes. Over the years, Eva has accepted her life with all its incompleteness. She has come to terms with the missing pieces, albeit painfully. But in her heart, a childish pining for her mother has never ceased. She is overcome with grief at the very mention of her mother and the last time he saw her with her hands stretched out to the little Eva, but unable to reach them.

The horrors of concentration camps cannot be written in mere words. One cannot begin to fathom the brutal realities the Jews suffered at the hands of the Nazis. Doctor Joseph Mengele was so vicious that he earned the sobriquet "Angel of Death". He conducted inhuman experiments on young children, stripping them naked, injecting tubes, and syringes into one hand, drawing blood samples from the other hand. For hours on end, these nightmarish experiments carried on and the children shuddered at the thought of having to line up for Mengele's visits and examination. With a scale, he would measure every inch of their body, drawing conclusions, seeing how his experiments to breed the "perfect race" of Germans were effective. Hitler's orders were clear. The aged, the disabled, the gays, the retarded were all directly walked to gas chambers. Frankl remembers vividly how Mengele supervised the segregation activities. Those sorted to the right were immediately walked to gas chambers to a horrifyingly painful death and the ones on the left were doomed to a treacherous life without their loved ones or any humane treatment. Soon after the sorting, the survivors were walked into a hall, asked to strip, and are shaved from head to toe. All possessions were forfeited, and a stamp of servitude is inked on the arm. They were stripped of their very identity, not allowed to even possess a name. Frankl's story cannot be complete without the mention of the horrors he went through along with the millions of Jews.

Lessons from Man's Search

Man's Search for meaning has touched and changed the lives of millions worldwide. Frankl wrote the book decades before depression and mental health were even a topic of discussion. Today, his book has only garnered more importance and profundity. Suicide rates have reached alarming levels and depression and mental problems have become a commonplace malaise, sparing no one, affecting the rich and poor, the ailing and the healthy alike. According to Frankl, people fail to find a reason for their existence and that is why their mental stability falters. People are ready to undergo any suffering if they know "why" they are suffering. The answer to the "why" is the purpose of one's life. Frankl calls it an "unheard cry for meaning".

Isn't that the real meaning of depression?

Find your Why...

To live a meaningless life can be frustrating to the core. People who fail to overcome that frustration take their life. In an interview conducted with Frankl, he says that the suicides in Auschwitz were an evaporating droplet compared to the suicides in a welfare state like Austria. The increasing case of suicides among teenagers is a growing crisis that needs to be addressed at the earliest. These youngsters have born with a silver spoon in their mouth and yet they are doing the heinous act of self-annihilation. Frankl says that teachers and parents share the blame because they have pampered so much that they become lackadaisical and depressed. Frankl stresses the importance of challenges in a youngster's life. He goes on to underscore that psychologist everywhere agree that placing too much stress is far less detrimental than placing too little pressure. When people are under-demanded, they tend to develop ennui towards every activity. They saunter about; their thoughts run wild. When there is a lot of time to bide away, people experience what Frankl calls the "existential vacuum" which in turn triggers "existential frustration". A sense of futility pervades all through their days which can be to the detriment of the very human nature to "do", "perform", and seek results and appreciation. Man is the only being in nature that is not driven only by his instinct or desire alone. In the modern world, even traditions don't inhibit or hold him back. Frankl warns that a person does what others do-which is conformism, or he does what others expect him to do-which is totalitarianism, both of which will stymie a person's individuality and personal progress. Frankl argues that both conformism and totalitarianism are the root cause of "existential vacuum".

What is the place of religion in finding meaning in life? Frankl agrees to the common belief that religion will aid in the process of finding meaning for life, but he also underscores that every man, irrespective of whether he is religious or not, can find the meaning of his life. And how can he do that- through work and love.

Frankl unambiguously says that our attitude towards our suffering is independent of the gravity of the situation. If anyone, but a Holocaust survivor had said this it would have been a bitter pill to swallow. In Frankl's case, the daily tortures and agonizing realities were weighing heavy on him. Having lost all of his family, Frankl was truly alone and devastated. What reason or purpose could he find in such dark times? But he kept his hopes alive by imagining the lectures he would be giving in the future about his experiences at the camp. Simply by changing that attitude, he saw that everything he suffered was objective. All this helped him to divert his attention from the morass of his present life to a liberated future when Frankl will be a free man with a career, maybe reunite with his loving wife.

"In some way, suffering ceases to be suffering at the moment it finds a meaning."

Frankl, like his two friends, managed to find meaning and so survived the camp's horrors. Everybody who survived the travesty of life in the concentration camp had something or someone to look forward to in the future. The others, who couldn't find any meaning or sense in their suffering perished before the liberation. When the Soviet men arrived to free the victims, they were appalled at the sight of these camps. Piles of dead bodies dotted the campus, with bodies at varying stages of putrefaction. It was an abominable scene straight from hell. There were mass graves where naked bodies were thrown in, spindly limbs lying haphazardly over one another. The sight was horrifying even for the war-hardened soldiers. The experiment rooms were rummaged and bodies of young children, with some of them limbless, were retrieved, and with shock and repugnance, they realized the Nazis had done vile things with the children. The world was exposed to one of the worst crimes against humanity.

Friedrich Nietzsche in circa 1875

Frankl was often seen quoting Friedrich Nietzsche's

(a German philosopher, poet, writer, and philologist) famous quote- "He who has a why to live for can bear almost any how."

Frankl was dejected and equally in despair. He ached to see his wife. He was stripped off his identity. But he noticed that he had an unrelenting passion to continue living no matter what. This uncanny ability to find meaning despite the dire situation he was in saw him through all the horrors of the camp. He noticed the same survival streak in other inmates. The inmates could be categorized into two groups. The ones who had lost all hope in humanity and had no faith in liberation or a future and the others that saw their life in the camp as a challenge to surmount. The latter group had a way to live the drudgery and so they survived despite the excruciating hunger pangs, the debilitating illness, and the mental and physical torture. Frankl deduced that among the few hardy survivors of the concentration camp were one common trait, all of them had some reason to hold on. They overcame all hurdles because of that one why. Fortunately, for Frankl, he belonged to that group. He too had a why and so he survived all the how's. In life too, there are umpteen challenges, and those who succeed in finding a why will survive all odds and come out of it successfully. If you are in a deep crisis, ask yourself, what is your why you will find the answer to the how is an answer to the why.

When the pandemic is reeling on unabated, thousands all over the world have suffered and are still suffering losses of one kind or the other. Loss of a loved one, loss of livelihood, material, and financial losses, and the list is endless. Children too are suffering enormously with schools and parks shut, they are leading drab, cloistered lives. This takes a toll on their mental psyche too. The ubiquitous suffering is unbearable but if one could discern the why then every hardship will cease to be suffering, argues Frankl. Frankl started observing all that he suffered in the camp as a learning process. In every subjugation, he sought a reason, in every humiliation, a purpose, in every pain, a lesson. That is how he arrived at the epiphanic truth that

For Frankl, every day was a challenge he had to overcome. He saw surviving each day as his task and he resolutely decided not to turn his back to the task. Every night he made himself tougher and readier for the task the next day. Slowly, he began to see opportunities for personal achievements. He got his "why". Like Frankl, can we also find the meaning in our toughest situation rather than wallow in self-pity? Can we too accept unpleasant situations as a challenge, take a course of action then sit, and whine about it? Convicts who sit just a few days away from electric chairs have told Frankl that they have found meaning in life. On the other hand, millionaires are killing themselves because they fail to find meaning.

This is how Frankl landed at the third branch of psychotherapy-logotherapy. Logotherapy dwells on meaning and not an introspective or retrospective analysis of oneself. It focuses singularly on the meanings of every situation, of life in general. What is the use of meekly surrendering to all happenings in life without being able to attach any meaning or purpose to it? Do you believe in fate or destiny? What is life is what you make it and not something scribbled on your head before you were born. Like the Indian mystic, Sadhguru has rightly said fate is destiny unattended. Destiny is when you take charge of your life. Fate happens to you when you leave your life to the natural progression of time. Sheer boredom can create enormous frustration in one's being. If you are frustrated with your life, it is because you have not yet found the meaning of your life or existence. It is this frustration that drives a person to depression and anxiety issues. The aim of logotherapy is not to cure an illness. It exists to aid you to find your meaning in life. It is only a guide to your hunt for the treasure of life. The journey of life is in the end one's own responsibility. This pursuit of a purpose can be frustrating and onerous. It can bring forth inner turmoil and may not be fruitful in the very first attempt. As human beings, it is incumbent on us to not give up the pursuit at the first brush with failure but relentlessly pursue it. It is akin to struggling to achieve something. What is the purpose of your existence? What is the driving force in your life? Are you living just because you are born or are you just passing through mundanities when night segues today and vice versa?

You Always Have a Choice!

There is always a choice. We feel there isn't any because of our myopic vision. Our prejudices stymie our thought process. Frankl argues in his book that between stimulus and response, there exists a gap, and in that gap, each one of us can decide our response. The universe is not within our control. There will always be external factors that act on our lives, creating situations that are not in our favor. There is no point in fretting about the traffic jam or the capricious weather, or in the present situation a pandemic. None of these events are in our control. However, how we respond to each of them is very much within our power. It is our choice to whether freak out or to stoically accept or take it as a challenge. Frankl was incarcerated in the grimmest situations a man can think of. Sitting in that hellish place where survivors say they could smell evil, Frankl managed to find hope. He argues that when external forces are beyond our power, internal forces are very much within our control. How our reaction to any given action is totally our choice. Nobody can take the freedom of your choice of reaction from you. Not even Hitler!

If a man can change the world, then he can change himself too. The circumstances cannot be altered but our responses can. Are you suffering from depression? Did you lose your job or did your marriage end? Are you suffering from a loveless marriage or a child-less one? Are you suffering from a terminal illness? Still, Frankl courageously declares that you can still find meaning and be content. When a man is no longer able to change a situation, he is challenged to change himself.

Man is far more resilient than he realizes

Frankl has had people sitting in dingy prisons talk

to him about how content and happy they are. We have been conditioned to believe that only if we have certain parameters of life then we shall be happy. Frankl says that medical textbooks can lie. For example, it is stated that man cannot exist without sleeping for a particular number of hours. If that were true, argues Frankl, he would have survived Auschwitz. He vividly describes the first night in Auschwitz. Every inmate had to sleep directly on wooden barracks with not a blanket over their debilitated bodies. Nine men had to cram themselves on each tier and only two blankets were given. Frankl says how the inmates were unable to clean their teeth and despite the severe vitamin deficiencies, they still had strong gums. The same shirts had to be worn every single day for one and a half years. During winters, taking a bath was out of the question because of frozen water pipes. Because of the will to survive, Frankl says that despite the scant washing and cleaning, their sores, and abrasions on the body, dirty from working for long in soil didn't worsen or catch an infection. The point Frankl puts across is that human beings are not delicate darlings but immensely resilient. Human resilience is astounding. Against all odds, he can emerge victorious, given he has the willpower.

Taking responsibility

Frankl suggests that the first thing that every man need is the right attitude in life. What we expected from life was not as consequential as what life expected of us. Finding the purpose in life is our responsibility. Life in itself is taking that responsibility to find that answer. Each one of us has a destiny, a journey. That journey may be replete with hurdles and problems. As intelligent beings, it is incumbent on each of us to seek answers and scale hurdles.

Face your fears

Fears are a part of our very emotional make-up. Each one of us has a fear or two. Logotherapy suggests facing the fears head-on. Like in the Harry Potter series, where the professor suggests that the best way to repel the monster is by ridiculing them. Similarly, attach a ridiculing situation to your fears and that will help diminish the enormity of the event, thus assuaging your anxiety. A paradoxical wish is what Frankl suggests. This technique lets one detach oneself from the fear and thus distance oneself from one's nemesis. Logotherapy focuses on fears in a two-prong method where our fear makes us anxious about a situation and that hyper-tension will make it impossible for achieving what one wishes. The day we learn to laugh at our fears we will find the cure to both hypertension and anxiety.

Everybody's why is different

In today's world where ubiquitous social media has made it impossible to keep anything private, peer pressure is at an all-time high. With every success story out in the open, people feel inadequate or left out if they don't have a similar success story to flaunt. Buying an expensive automobile, vacationing at exotic places, career, or personal achievements, everything is publicized with great fanfare and aplomb. The ones who are still struggling to get that degree or get a decent job or a happy love life may feel insecure and inadequate. They might feel they are living pitiful lives without even a semblance of success. There may be women who experienced miscarriages and they see their colleagues or friends celebrating the birth of a second or even third child, imagine the stress and pain that will creep into their minds inadvertently. But if one could just understand that not every man's destiny is alike. Every one of us has different journeys. This is what Frankl says that no man and no destiny can be compared with another man or his destiny.

Frankl pleads his readers not to compare themselves to another. Other people's milestones might not be yours and it is perfectly ok. Nothing is more futile than comparing one's life with another's. Even in suffering, every man is unique and almost always alone in this universe. Every man's unique opportunity lies within him, in the way he bears his suffering.

Importance of Love in our lives

Frankl says that human beings can attain the highest form of their being only through love and in love. It is the only way to grasp another human being in the very uniqueness of his being, the innermost core of his individuality. Frankl projects love as an antidote to all pain. When the Nazi guards were cruel and brutal to him and his fellow inmates, Frankl would fill his mind with images of his wife. The love of his wife made him survive the odious camp. His tormented mind had clung on to the image of his wife. He says in detail how he imagined her with an "uncanny acuteness". He could hear her answering him, saw her smiling at him from the gossamer mist of pre-dawn hours. Frankl could see her genuine and love-filled look. At that moment, in the darkest hours, Frankl felt that her smile was more luminous than the rising sun.

Frankl underscores the timeless adage-Love conquers all. In that epiphanic moment, Frankl grasped the very meaning of the greatest secret that all poetry and prose, human thought and belief have tried to impart for eons that man's salvation was in love and through love alone. Frankl realized with great joy that even a man like him who lost everything in his life and had no hope to live for could still be happy even if it was for an infinitesimal moment. And how did he achieve it? Simply by visualizing the image of his beloved, by conjuring up her blissful face in the very depths of his mind. That is when Frankl understood that despite the odds, and in spite of all hardships and despair, when a man can no longer bring himself into positive action, at that time, by simple contemplation of his most loved one can aid in him achieving fulfillment. Since a person is not his physical being, Frankl espouses that if we love a person deeply then it is his spiritual being, his innermost self that we love and so whether he is alive or not, that ceases to matter at all.

Don't pursue happiness and success

In his book Man's Search for Meaning, Frankl stresses the importance of not pursuing happiness or success. He underscores that pursuing success or happiness is a chimerical task. The more you try to aim at success, the more the chances that you will miss it. The more you make happiness a target, the more the chances that you will miss it. Just like happiness cannot be pursued, success too should ensue. Get a greater cause, remain devoted to it, and success will and should only be a side-effect of that relentless dedication. Happiness should be a by-product of one's complete surrender to a cause that is greater than one's own self. Happiness, according to Frankl, must happen. The same applies to success. By not caring about success, by not making happiness a target or a destination, one can achieve it in the most glorious ways. This philosophy is akin to the one expiated in the Bhagavad Gita, the holy book of Hinduism, which states that do your dharma without attachment to the fruits of it. Bhagavad Gita exhorts Hindus to do one's duties without worrying or thinking of the fruits of their labor. According to the Holy Scripture, man is bound to do his duties ceaselessly, not letting his situations influence his devotion to duty.

Pursuing happiness or success is a foolhardy mission. Shut out all the noises of the outer world and sit at peace with yourself and your surroundings. Slowly, and inevitably, a feeble voice will begin to emerge from within your being. That whisper can be heard only when you let it be heard. That whisper is your consciousness. Whatever it tells you to do, do it with all your heart, to the best of your knowledge, without worrying about its results, without letting its fruits weigh you down. One must not let anything affect one's peace of mind. I realize that it is easier said than done. The onerous task here is to shut out your own thoughts, those hammering thoughts that eat at your inner peace inexorably. It seems unstoppable but it is only powerful until you take command of your thoughts. By taking command of one's mind, one can master one's thoughts as well. Thoughts, like emotions, should not be let loose. Be the master of your thoughts and don't succumb to be its slave. When such a situation arises, anxiety creeps in, choking the soul and mind alike. Anxiety and hypertension thrive in a negative environment. Once you pursue your work devotedly, without attachment to fruits, and then, in the long run, success will follow only because, Frankl says, "you forgot about it".

Cherishing one's memories..

Life wouldn't be worth living if it wasn't for our memories. It is both a blessing and a curse, they say. A blessing because our sweet memories help us revisit the good old times we had, a curse because a painful memory can hurt for a very long time. Frankl draws a comparison to drive home his ideas pertinent to memories. He says when a pessimist looks at his calendar and worries about how he is losing day every time he tears a sheet. But a man who had not given himself to slovenliness and had taken the challenges of each day head-on will remove every sheet from his calendar with the same alacrity with which he had at the beginning of the day, and he would carefully file it away with the previous sheets. At the back, he would have scribbled a few lessons he learned that day. In retrospect he can look at these notes, enriched with the goodness and knowledge of experience, and feel proud of his accomplishment. For him, he is living every day to the fullest. The thought of "losing" a day doesn't even cross his mind. Frankl poses questions to his reader asking them for such a man devoted to his duties, will the fact that he is growing old scare him. Or will he look at the youthful younger generation with envy? And then Frankl himself attempts to answer the rhetoric. Such a man is an accomplished one. He will prefer his "realities of past" to the "possibilities" of a future he doesn't have. Frankl explains further that such a man shall not only be happy and content with his "work done", and "love loved", but he shall also be proud of "sufferings suffered" courageously. And then Frankl goes on to explain why he is proud of his own life and the way he suffered bravely all his losses, and sufferings.

Frankl admits that none of what he suffered will evoke envy, considering the horrors of the Nazi extermination camp.

What is the true meaning of life

Frankl has told umpteen times the importance of finding meaning in life. He goes on to elaborate that the true meaning is not limited within the shackles of one's physical being, but one must go into the outer world and try harnessing all that one can. He terms such an enterprising approach "self-transcendence of human existence". It is human instinct to always be pointed, directed to someone or something. He opines that the more a man devotes himself to another being or a cause, the more humane he becomes. Self-actualization, Frankl says is not achievable because the more one tries to capture it, the more the chance to miss it. It is only achievable as a side-effect of self-transcendence.

The Journey to Logotherapy

Viktor Frankl was born as the second child of Grabriel Frankl who was a civil servant in the Ministry of Social Service and Elsa. Frankl had a penchant for psychology from an early age itself. He pursued night classes on applied psychology while he was still in junior high school. Even as a teenager, he interacted with Sigmund Freud. Soon after graduating high school, Frankl studied medicine in 1923 at the University of Vienna. He specialized in neurology and psychiatry that mainly centered on depression and self-annihilation. The following year, The International Journal of Psychoanalysis published his first scientific study. Frankl was the president of the Social Democratic Party of Austria's youth consortium for high school goers. This is when he grew skeptical of the Freudian approach in Psychotherapy. He was eventually led to Alfred Adler's student followers. This meeting was instrumental in Frankl publishing his second paper Psychotherapy and Worldview. He was resuscitated by Adler's team when he vociferously espoused that meaning was a central motivational force in every human being. Adler, as stated before focuses on the will to better others as the driving force in man. It wasn't late before Frankl developed his own branch called logotherapy. By 1926, he had begun working on the third branch of psychotherapy. Frankl was so passionate about healing others of their mental fatigue that he organized youth counseling campaigns even when he was still a student. The increasing number of teen suicides was what prompted him to start counseling centers in 1928. It was under state sponsorship and all services were provided for gratis. Frankl made sure that the patients had the best services of other competent psychologists like Charlotte Buhler and Erwin Wexberg. The surprising impact of counseling sessions was that not a single student's life was lost to suicide during the whole year in

1931.

In 1930, he completed his MD and started working at Steinhof Psychiatric Hospital. Frankl's patients were women who had suicidal tendencies. After seven years, he started to practice privately. The following year, the Nazi rampage had begun, and it stymied his efforts to treat the patients. Hitler had annexed Austria. Things were soon going downhill, for Jews. By 1940, only one hospital admitted Jews, the Rothschild Hospital. Frankl began working there as the head of the Neurology department. The Nazis were coming down heavily on all mentally ill people. Frankl did all in his capacity to help patients escape the euthanasia program that Hitler rampantly carried out. Time was running out for him. In 1942, both Frankl and his wife were deported to concentration camps. They had been married only for nine months then. His father would die at Theresienstadt concentration camp after catching tenacious pneumonia and starvation. Two years later, Frankl along with his surviving family was shifted to Auschwitz. Tragically, his mother and brother were eventually killed in the gas chambers. His wife would die of typhus in the Bergen-Belsen concentration camp. Frankl has survived the horrors of four different concentration camps in three years.

Bergen Belsen Concentration camp in 1945

Mass graves at Bergen Belsen

The last concentration camp being burned down

Anne Frank memorial at Bergen Belsen camp

Post Liberation life

Soon after liberation by the Red Army, Frankl became the head of the neurology department at a hospital and also started a private practice. Within three years after being liberated, Frankl had earned his Ph.D. in philosophy. His dissertation, titled, The Unconscious God, studied the relation between psychology and religion. He continued healing patients until he retired in 1970. Frankl supports the idea of using Socratic dialogue to discover the "unconscious" within. In 1955, he was awarded a professorship at the University of Vienna in neurology and psychiatry. All through his career, Frankl dispelled reductionist tendencies in early psychoanalysis. He argued that these approaches dehumanized a patient. He was awarded the Oskar Pfister Award by American Psychiatric Association in 1985.

Soon after liberation, having lost all his family to

the gas chambers, Frankl was overcome with grief. He returned to Vienna a devastated and extremely impoverished man. Despite the grief and the debilitating physical illness, he set himself to the task of writing the manuscript that was destroyed by Hitler's brown shirts. In less than ten days, he wrote Man's Search for Meaning. It was initially titled "A Psychologist Experiences the Concentration Camp." Release in 1946, it was initially published in the German language. Millions were lost, facing the same mental conundrum and existential crisis as Frankl and maybe that is why the book sold in millions. The English translation was published in 1959. The book's success made Frankl realize the "mass neurosis" of our times. The book title promised to address the problem of finding the meaningfulness of one's life. The book featured as the most influential book in the States.

In 1941, while working at Rothschild Hospital, Frankl met his wife Tilly Grosser. She was a station nurse. Soon after the two got married, Tilly had become pregnant but due to some medical reasons, Tilly had to undergo an abortion. Once shifted to Bergen Belsen camp, Frankl never saw Tilly again. His wife has been the driving force in his life. He has cited her as the reason for him surviving all hardships in his life at the camp. His aged father too had died of starvation at the ghetto for Jews in 1943. He was 81 at that time. His sister, Stella had managed to escape to Australia. Later in 1947, Frankl married Eleonore Katharina. She was a catholic. Frankl and Elly visited both church and synagogues, respecting each other's religion, celebrating Christmas and Hanukkah with equal vigor. They had only one daughter named Gabriele. Gabriele walked in her father's footsteps becoming a child psychologist. Frankl lived a happy and fulfilling life despite all that he suffered in the camp. He went through all trauma with courage and finally graced higher abodes on 2nd September 1997 due to a heart attack. His mortal remains are buried in Vienna Central Cemetery.

Viktor Frankl, the greatest healer of the human mind of all times has riveted generations of readers, young and old alike with the chilling details of horrors of concentration camps and his lessons for spiritual survival. Here is a man who suffered the death of his entire family, went through nightmarish hell in four different concentration camps, and yet was thinking selflessly of helping humanity. He had turned all his sufferings into a personal triumph simply by making full use of all his experiences for the betterment of his own life and the lives of millions of others. No one is spared from suffering. Not even the most influential and the richest people on the earth. If money, fame, or even success could bring happiness, then we wouldn't have heard stories of billionaires killing themselves. Despite all the technological advancements, people are so lonely. They are constantly in search of something, but they are oblivious to what is it that they are searching for. Those who pursue happiness in success know well that chasing one peak will only make you realize that there are umpteen other peaks to be conquered.

Frankl says that underestimating a man will only make him fail, because of crosswinds. By overestimating a man, we always help him achieve what he can achieve in life. Frankl believes in the aim of the sky to reach the stars. In that sense, he explains that the idealists are the actual realists because only they reach their true potential. This forms the maxim and motto of his psychotherapy. Frankl describes the story of a fellow inmate who had believed deeply in his heart that he would be free by March 30th. That man dreamt of the day when he will finally walk out as a free man. He was so convinced that March 30th was his day of liberation, that he forgot all woes that his life was steeped in. March 30th came and went, but nothing happened. The man was devastated. He couldn't come to terms with the depressing reality that he was stuck in the same misery of life. He eventually died much before the Soviet army came to liberate the Jews. Frankl says that the man eventually caught some disease and that his body succumbed to its vileness. But would he have survived the illness had he will not be broken? That is the question that Frankl exhorts his readers to seek answers for.

As far as Frankl is concerned, he found peace and tranquility with the image of his life. He illustrates a day in the camp when they were working in a trench, starving themselves to death. Everywhere Frankl looked he could see only greyness, both figuratively and literary. The dawn was a lugubrious grey; a paling grey hung over the monotonous sky, the snow looked grey in the shimmering light of the sun, the rags they were clad in was a dirty greyish color, and their blood-drained faces looked grey. He imagined conversing with his wife. He knew his life was nothing but a slow and extremely painful death. Conjuring the image of his loving wife was only his heart's desperate way of clinging on to hope in all its hopelessness. He was desperate to find a meaning for his sufferings. He saw none. It was increasingly becoming impossible to see it. Seeking meaning when you are immersed in a bottomless pit of suffering and pain feels like a chimerical pursuit. Frankl saw the hopelessness of imminent death hanging thick in the greyness all around. He looked at his fellow mates, they looked famished, and their limbs bare skeletons, their eyes devoid of all life and hope. They had lost all vestiges of being a human. None of them seemed to have even an iota of hope that something good will ever happen to them again. But, despite the odds, something stirred within him and he realized that his spirit was beginning to shake away its greyness, and be born again. Frankl felt that his rejuvenated spirit could transcend the enveloping hopelessness. As if taking a cue, as if the universe was giving him a sign, a light from a distance farmhouse came alive on the horizon. Frankl compares it to a painting amidst all the greyness of the Bavarian dawn. Like the sun's rays were piercing through the looming greyness, Frankl's spirit was shining through the engulfing darkness of his soul. For hours, he stood in the freezing greyness plowing through the icy snow-clad ground. The brown shirts passed, and they flung profanities at the working men. Frankl chose to look away and engage in communicating with his wife. He felt as though he could touch her when she was within his embrace. His feelings were so strong that he couldn't understand the intense life force within. It was as if his spirit was reasserting itself on him. At that moment, Frankl saw a bird had flown down; it sat on the little hill of soil he had been working on. The bird seemed to look at him piercingly. Humor according to Frankl, is another important weapon in self-preservation. In the end, all of Frankl's teachings can be summarized like this: find meaning in life- a purposeful work, find love, and finally find the courage to face all odds.

Extras

Author's Request

Our books are intended to indulge you. If you enjoyed this book or gained any valuable information from it in any way, feel free to share your experience with us. Your contented reviews will help to boost us not only in the sales perspective but also to improve our creativity. Please leave a review at the store front where you purchased this book, and it would be greatly appreciated.

Made in the USA
Middletown, DE
21 June 2022